YOUR MIND MATTERS

SOCIAL MEDIA AND YOU

Honor Head

W
FRANKLIN WATTS
LONDON • SYDNEY

First published in Great Britain in 2019
by The Watts Publishing Group
10 9 8 7 6 5 4 3 2 1
All rights reserved

Editor: Nicola Edwards
Cover design: Lisa Peacock and Thy Bui
Inside design: Matthew Lilly
Cover and inside illustrations
by Roberta Terracchio
Consultant: Ellie Proffitt, Education Manager at Childnet
International (https://www.childnet.com)

ISBN 978 1 4451 6473 1 (HB); 978 1 4451 6474 8 (PB)
Printed in China

FSC
www.fsc.org
MIX
Paper from
responsible sources
FSC® C104740

Franklin Watts
An imprint of
Hachette Children's Group
Part of the Watts Publishing Group
Carmelite House
50 Victoria Embankment
London EC4Y 0DZ
An Hachette UK Company
www.hachette.co.uk
www.franklinwatts.co.uk

WHAT IS A TRUSTED ADULT?

Throughout the book we suggest you speak to a trusted adult. This is a person who makes you feel safe and that you can trust. It could be a parent or carer or another family member, such as an aunt or uncle or grandparent. It could be a teacher or someone you know well, such as a family friend or a friend's parent or carer. Or it could be someone at the end of a helpline (see pages 46-47).

CONTENTS

Social media, it's great, right? 4

Social media and your brain 7

Oh, no! FOMO! 10

Exclusion zone 13

Please like me! 16

Not real life 19

Body image 22

Developing self-worth 25

Cyberbullying 28

Sleep well 31

Online help 34

Take a tech break 37

The last word – selfies! 40

Glossary 42

Notes for teachers, parents and carers 44

Further information 46

Index 48

SOCIAL MEDIA, IT'S GREAT, RIGHT?

Social media can be brilliant for keeping in touch with friends and family, for doing homework research and finding out who's doing what where. But it's important to balance your online life with your offline life.

LIFE ONLINE

The time we spend online is linked to our physical and mental health, which affects how we think, feel and behave. We need to learn how to use social media in a fun and safe way and not let it become a habit that can take over and make us feel unhappy and anxious.

BE AWARE

Social media can cause all sorts of problems that happen before we know it. One of the worst of these is cyberbullying. In real life we can see how someone reacts to something we say or do, but online, we can't. When you can't see how someone is reacting to something you say, or how they are feeling, it might seem that it doesn't matter what you say. But by joining in with nasty comments that make fun of someone, you can make them feel scared, upset and hurt. And if you're the one being cyberbullied it can make your life a misery. We'll look at ways to beat cyberbullying later in this book.

5

PERFECT PEOPLE

We all love to see what everyone's wearing, where they are and who they're with. However, if we keep seeing pictures of people looking fabulous, and having an amazing time, it might make us feel as if we're missing out. We could become jealous and unhappy with what we have. It can make us feel that we're not good enough just being who we are, and think we have to be like the perfect people we see online.

To get the best out of social media you have to make sure that you stay in control, rather than let it control you. You can do this by remembering that most people only show the best bits of their life online and what you see online is not always how it really is at all.

TRY THIS!

Look out for these boxes throughout the book. They will give hints and tips on quick ways to improve your mental health that you can do every day or whenever you need to.

SOCIAL MEDIA AND YOUR BRAIN

Scientists, doctors and psychologists are doing lots of research to find out how social media and the use of digital devices affect the way people, especially young people, think and feel.

ALWAYS ONLINE

Your brain is changing and growing rapidly all the time. It can be affected in all sorts of ways by too much screen time, which includes television, computers, tablets and mobile phones. Scientific studies have proved that spending too long on digital devices can be bad for mental and physical development in young people. It's tricky to say how much time is too much as it will vary from person to person. You just need to make sure that your offline life doesn't suffer because of the time you spend being online.

POSITIVES AND NEGATIVES

In 2018, the Safer Internet Centre did a survey of 2,000 8- to 17-year-olds, asking how social media affected them. Well over half said that chatting to friends online cheered them up and that in the past week they had seen something online that had made them feel inspired, excited and happy.

However, nearly half said that being online had made them feel sad, worried and anxious and that they had experienced mean comments or been excluded online. When social media goes well it can make you feel good and supported, but when it goes badly it can cause negative feelings and even lead to depression.

THE EFFECTS OF DEPRESSION

Depression is a serious mental illness that can make people feel sad and hopeless. It makes someone lose interest in their friends, family, hobbies, themselves – everything. Depression causes lack of concentration and makes people find it really hard to do even simple everyday tasks.

HOW CAN SOCIAL MEDIA CAUSE DEPRESSION?

Young people are using social media more and more to develop friendships, discover what they feel about themselves and others and learn about the world around them. However, they are also judging themselves by what happens online more than anything else.

They can start to obsess about online 'friends' and think they themselves are only clever/pretty/cool if people online 'like' them and praise them. All this stress to compete can be exhausting, make people feel lonely and isolated, cause a negative self-image and lead to some people experiencing anxiety and depression.

OH, NO! FOMO!

Using social media to keep in touch with what's going on and what your friends are up to is great, but sometimes it can take over.

FEAR OF MISSING OUT

Social media helps to keep you in the loop about what is going on … the latest funny video, shopping trip or chat about your favourite vlogger or sports club. Wanting to be part of what's going on is perfectly natural, but if you feel that you have to be online all the time so you don't miss out on any group chat, messaging, or invite, you could be experiencing FOMO – Fear of Missing Out.

FACE-TO-FACE V. ONLINE

* Think about why and if you really need to be online so much.

* Are you enjoying your time online?

* Are you missing out on face-to-face time with friends and family?

* Does being online make you feel happy or does it sometimes feel like something you have to do to keep your friends happy?

* Is it making you feel tired and anxious?

KEEP IT FUN

When being online stops being fun don't let it become a problem. It might be time to cut down on social media if:

* you spend more time with friends online than with friends in person

* you feel you need to be available online all the time to stay popular and keep your friends

* you think you might lose friends if you don't answer a message or text immediately.

These feelings can make you feel stressed and out of control, and this can lead to low self-esteem (how you value yourself). Take a deep breath, and take control of the situation. Here are some ideas to help you fight the FOMO:

✱ Plan how to cut back your hours online. Tell your friends that you are only going to be online at certain times of the day – say an hour in the afternoon and an hour in the evening, but not just before bedtime (see page 33).

✱ Instead of online chat, make a date to meet up in person. Visit friends at home, go for an ice-cream or take a picnic to the park.

TRY THIS!

Think about why you feel you might be missing out. Is it pressure being put on you by other people online, or pressure you are putting on yourself? Write down why you feel stressed about social media; sometimes writing down your worries and anxieties can make them seem less frightening and overwhelming.

EXCLUSION ZONE

Being deliberately left out of chats, games and messaging can be shocking and upsetting for the person who is being excluded.

BEING IGNORED

It can be really hard if you are suddenly left out of chats and games, stop getting 'likes', are ignored online and not messaged by anyone. If this is happening to you, think about why it may have happened. Might your friends be reacting to something you've said online? It is so easy to respond quickly to a message or chat that sometimes the words come out wrong. And sometimes people can misread what someone has said and think they're being unkind, when they don't mean to be.

When we talk face-to-face we have people's facial expressions and body language to help us understand what is being said. Of course online we can't see people so we only have the words, and by themselves they can be misread. If you think this might have happened, ask a friend at school. If you have upset someone without realising it, explain it was a mistake. It is very brave to admit to your mistakes and good friends will understand if you did upset them by mistake.

MOVE ON

Social media exclusion that happens over a long time is a form of cyberbullying that is intended to upset someone and make them feel bad about themselves. Being excluded online can make people feel alone, confused, sad and anxious. If this is happening to you, try switching off your social media for a while. The bullies will soon get bored. Set up new messaging groups with friends you trust or text people individually. Talk to your friends about what is happening and arrange to meet up in real life when they can give you all the latest news in person. If your friends don't seem to care, perhaps you need to think about making new friends who do care about how you feel.

WHY ME?

Don't think it's your fault if you are excluded. People who exclude you online on purpose are not being good friends. Keep positive, remember all your good qualities and share your friendship with the friends that are always there for you.

> *I felt really terrible when I was suddenly ignored online. I thought I was a bad person.... There had to be a reason why no one was talking to me. Then a friend told me someone had been spreading rumours about me that weren't true because they were jealous of me. That made me feel sad but it also made me feel better that it wasn't about me, but about how the other person felt. I stayed off instant messaging for a while anyway and I didn't really miss it.*
>
> Sam, 14

PLEASE LIKE ME!

Studies have shown that more and more young people judge themselves by the likes and comments they get from others on social media.

LIKING BEING LIKED

Wanting to be liked is nothing new. Because humans are social creatures we all need to feel that we are liked and wanted by those people that matter to us – our family, friends and close schoolmates. But social media has taken being liked and accepted to a new level. Now we want everyone to 'like' us, even people we don't know.

THE SCIENCE BIT

Experts have discovered that when we see someone has 'liked' us or when we get a positive comment online, this creates feelings of joy and happiness in the brain. These feelings only last for a short while, and they can become addictive. This means we need more and more likes and great comments to feel happy.

BREAKING THE HABIT

If we rely on 'likes' to feel good about ourselves, and then stop getting them, or not enough of them, it can damage our self-esteem. We might begin to think we are worthless or not good enough, or stupid and ugly.

STEP AWAY

If this is happening to you, it may be you need to step away and take a break from social media and just stay in touch with close friends and family instead. Start thinking about yourself in a more positive way rather than relying on other people to boost your confidence.

Try a new hobby or join a group to get better at something you already enjoy, such as singing, painting, drama or sport. Being addicted to 'likes' is being recognised as a real problem so it is nothing to be ashamed of. But don't keep waiting for others to like you. Remember that you are more than good enough just the way you are.

TRY THIS!

If you feel you are losing confidence because you aren't getting enough 'likes' or good feedback on your postings, try some positive thinking. Take a few minutes every day to like yourself! When you're cleaning your teeth, getting dressed or walking to the bus stop, recite five great things about yourself. You might have lovely shiny hair, make the best sandwiches, help with the chores at home or be brilliant at football or art. Can't think of five things? Ask your family and close friends.

NOT REAL LIFE

It may seem obvious, but what happens on social media is not the same as in real life. People's lives in photos, blogs, tweets and videos can all be made to seem far more perfect than they are in reality.

WANTING MORE

Experts have found that when we see people online wearing the latest clothes, looking amazing and out with their mates doing fun things, it can have a negative impact on our mental health. It can make us feel dissatisfied with what we've got and keep us always wanting more. We get to a point where we will never be satisfied with what we have because someone online will always have something newer, more expensive or better. This can make us envious, unhappy and stressed.

FEELING LONELY

Humans are social, we like to mix with other humans, but social media is almost the opposite of that. It's great at keeping us in touch with one another, but if people are glued to their digital devices they're not interacting with others face-to-face. Spending too much time on social media can make us feel lonely even if we have loads of online friends. Also, seeing photos online of people having fun together or reading about what everyone else is doing, can sometimes make us feel isolated and alone.

SPOT THE SIGNS
Do you:

* constantly compare yourself to your friends

* compare your achievements – how well or badly you've done – by what others have achieved

* think everyone else is having a better time than you

* lie awake at night worrying about how you can make your life more like those you see online?

Whatever you see online, remember that no one has a perfect life – everyone has both good and bad times. Most of us (even you, probably!) choose to put the best bits of our life on social media and ignore the boring, dull or unhappy bits. Don't be taken in; take control and make a plan to do more away from social media. Join a club or make a regular date to meet friends for a game or a chat. Or see what the rest of the family is doing and join in.

TAKE ACTION

Rather than worry about what you haven't got or what you wish you had, focus on what you do have and how you can achieve what you want. If you have a burning ambition to be like someone online, whether it's a singer, a sports star or a scientist, make a plan about how you can achieve this. No one is successful without a lot of hard work, even if they make it look easy online.

BODY IMAGE

Body image is what people think of their bodies and how they see themselves when they look in the mirror.

ALL CHANGE

As you grow your body will change, especially when you start to go through puberty. You might become aware of getting more hair on your body or your body shape changing. You might begin to compare how you look with your friends and with people you admire on social media. If someone feels that they don't look as good as people online this can begin to affect their self-esteem and their body image. They might think they are too tall, too short, too fat or too thin, for example.

TRICKS OF THE TRADE

Bloggers and celebrities spend hours putting on make-up, getting the lighting right or preparing a single shot to look absolutely perfect. They use filters and photo-editing apps and can take hundreds of photos before getting the one that is just right. In real life they probably don't look anything like as cool as they do online.

There is no perfect body shape or perfect way to look. We are all different and we should be proud of that.

CARE, BUT BE AWARE

It's perfectly natural to care about how you look, but if you find yourself obsessing about your appearance and feel unhappy about it all the time, you could have a negative body image. People who feel really unhappy about how they look may be more likely to suffer from eating disorders such as bulimia, anorexia or binge eating. If you feel this is happening to you, talk to a trusted adult, maybe a family member, a friend's mum or a teacher at school. Or ask your parents or carers to take you to see a doctor.

No one is going think any the worse of you because you asked for help. In fact you are being very grown up facing the problem and trying to do something about it.

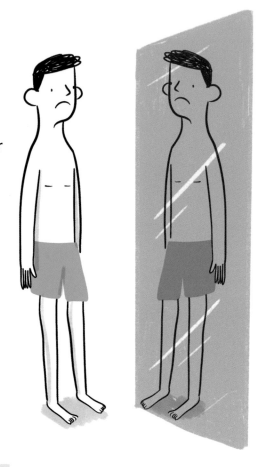

"

Online everyone looks so pretty with smooth skin. My skin was blotchy and I had freckles. Mum caught me putting on her foundation and asked why I needed it. I told her to cover up my freckles because they made me look ugly. She found a picture of one of my favourite singers without any make-up – and she had freckles! Now I see lots of models with freckles and it makes me feel better.

Anna, 11

"

DEVELOPING SELF-WORTH

Comparing yourself to
other people is never going to
make you feel good. You have
to learn to love who you are
and develop self-worth.

IT'S WORTH THE WORK

Self-worth is how
much you value and
respect yourself – your
body, your skills, your
personality, everything
about you.

Self-worth is being able to like who you are no matter what anyone else says about you. It's about being proud of who you are. A good body image is an important part of having a strong sense of self-worth. Some people may need to work harder than others to accept their body image, but it's well worth it. Do things you enjoy and that make you feel good about yourself and your life.

If you're following someone online who makes you feel miserable about how you look, unfollow them. Find another blog that focuses on skills and ideas rather than appearance. For example, look for sites that can help you improve your sporting skills or can teach you a new craft that you'll really enjoy.

ONLY HUMAN

Self-worth is not all about how you look. It's about realising that everyone is different and we all have lots of good points and a few not so good points – that's called being human! Good self-worth means feeling positive about yourself and your life. Spending too much time online comparing yourself to others is unlikely to help you develop your sense of self-worth.

ACHIEVE GREAT THINGS

Find blogs written by people who have achieved something special. This will give you inspiration and help spark creative ideas about how you can do great things. Go online to find out about interesting things happening in your area that might be something new for you to learn about or get involved with. Or find out about places to visit locally that you can go to with your family.

TRY THIS!

Think about new things to do offline and online. Plan a video call with a friend or family member you haven't seen for a long time. Organise a trip to the park for a game or a picnic with your best friend, family or a group of friends. Spending time with people we love and care about and that make us happy is one of the best ways to boost self-worth and keep us feeling positive.

CYBERBULLYING

Being bullied on a phone, website, app or game is cyberbullying and can have a serious effect on mental health.

HIDING BEHIND ANONYMITY

On games, messaging sites, social media sites and in chat rooms it is very easy to humiliate and threaten people, tell lies about people, start rumours and post embarrassing photos. Many people who wouldn't bully face-to-face feel safe bullying online as they can remain anonymous.

Cyberbullying can happen at any time of day or night – if it is happening to you it can feel like there is nowhere to hide. If you stick to friending just people you know personally and trust, there is less chance that you will be cyberbullied.

BLOCK THE BULLIES

Cyberbullying can make people withdrawn, anxious and depressed. It can affect their home life, schoolwork and friendships. In some cases it can lead to self-harming and suicide. If you are being cyberbullied on social media speak to a trusted adult about what is happening. Block or delete the person who is bullying you. If you're not sure what is abuse, and whether you should report it to the police, look at pages 46-47 for organisations you can contact for help.

IT'S SERIOUS

Everyone takes cyberbullying very seriously, including teachers. If one teacher can't help you, speak to someone else at school who can.

The school has a duty to make sure that there is nothing in your personal life that is damaging your ability to do your schoolwork or to be safe, happy and healthy. If you would prefer to talk safely to someone you don't know via a helpline, there are contact details on pages 46-47.

DON'T BE A BULLY

Think before you post on social media. It's easy to post a comment about a photo that you think is funny but it could upset the person whose photo it is. And it could result in other followers turning on you!

"

When I was being cyberbullied on social media my friends told me to ignore it but I couldn't think about anything else. Eventually I started just messaging my mates until everything calmed down. My mates were great about it... they would message me to let me know about changes to plans and where to meet. The bullying has stopped now, and I didn't miss being on social media as much as I thought I would.

Ravi, 14

"

SLEEP WELL

Social media platforms never switch off, but you need to. Sleep is important for everyone for good physical and mental health.

SLEEP – IT'S GOOD FOR YOU

Research shows that preteens need between 9 to 12 hours' sleep a night. This is not just grown-ups being, well, grown up, lack of sleep affects you physically and mentally. It can cause mood swings, make you feel anxious and grumpy, and unable to concentrate on schoolwork, and can lead to depression.

Not getting enough sleep means you don't really enjoy yourself when you're with your friends, either, because you may feel sleepy or be irritable with everyone or your brain may feel groggy.

SWEET DREAMS

During sleep your body repairs cells and releases growth hormones. It strengthens your immune system that keeps you physically healthy and your nervous system that keeps you feeling good. When we sleep we all dream (though sometimes we don't remember them when we wake up). Dreams are really important to our mental and physical health.

When we dream, our brain is helping us to sort through problems we had during the day and to come up with solutions. In this way, dreams can help us to deal with something that may have upset us during the day. Dreams can also help to turn our experiences into memories.

SWITCH OFF

Experiments have proved that the blue light from digital screens can affect our sleep cycles. It can also affect the quality of our sleep so that we feel groggy in the morning – not good if you've got a test or maths lesson first thing or an important sports game. You should switch off at least an hour before you go to sleep to let your brain adjust and make sure you get a really good night's sleep.

If you find you wake up and check your phone or tablet in the night, you need to take control of the situation and set yourself a nightly routine. Check all your messages an hour before bed and then leave the device downstairs or ask an adult in your household to keep it with them until morning.

ONLINE HELP

One of the best places to
go for help if you're having trouble
on social media, is ... online! There
are charities and specialist
websites that offer advice
and support.

SUPPORT AND UNDERSTANDING

Many charities have websites that help and support
young people having a tough time at home, school or
online. We've listed some on pages 46-47 and there might
be others local to your area, too. Do an online search for
a site specifically aimed at kids. Being scared and sad
can make you feel very alone. It can make you feel as if
you're the only person suffering or being threatened.

Online you can find advice and support and read
about how others who are the same age as you have
coped with similar experiences. Never agree to meet up
with anyone from online, and if someone suggests you
meet, tell an adult. Some charities also have counsellors
you can talk to.

They are specially trained to listen to you and give you support and advice. They will never be shocked or angry at what you say so you do not need to feel guilty, embarrassed or ashamed when talking to them. You can be honest and open.

CHATS AND PHONE CALLS

If you are worried about your thoughts, feelings or behaviour, joining an online group can be a great help in expressing how you feel, sharing your fears and worries and realising that you are not the only person going through a tough time. But you still need to be aware of online safety whilst finding help online. Don't ever post your name or any personal details, not even which school you go to.

> *When I went through a time when I was feeling really bad about myself, I rang a charity helpline. The lady I talked to was really understanding and helpful. It made me feel better to talk it through and know I wasn't the only one feeling this way.*
>
> Ned, 13

OFFLINE WORKS, TOO!

Sometimes people can feel that their negative thoughts and sad feelings are getting too much for them. If you ever feel like that, talking to someone you trust may help, but try to do this face-to-face if you can. Putting very personal stuff online about your deepest feelings and fears could lead to other people making nasty comments or trying to take advantage of how bad you feel. And talking in person is so much better anyway – you can't have a hug on the phone!

TAKE A TECH BREAK

Spending too much time
online or just fancy a change?
Why not give yourself and your
friends a tech break challenge?

START SOMETHING NEW

Being on social media all the time might stop you trying
out new things, such as an after-class sports club,
or make you feel cross and anxious when the family
suggest a weekend camping, for
example, where there are no digital
signals. If the idea of no tech
makes you feel really stressed,
a tech break could be exactly
what you need.

HOW MUCH IS TOO MUCH?

It is difficult to say how much time spent online is too much as it depends on the individual person, how they use social media and how social media affects them. Here are some signs to look out for:

* Do you believe you can't cope without social media?

* Do you feel anxious and panicky when you're not online?

* Do you stay awake at night so you can check messages and social sites during the night?

* Is your schoolwork suffering because of your social media life?

* Do you lie about how much time you spend online?

* Would you rather be online than with family and friends?

If you feel worried about how you're handling social media, talk to an adult you trust about how you are feeling. They can help you manage how you spend your time online. Don't think that what you're feeling is silly or trivial or not worth worrying anyone about. Social media is a powerful force and sometimes we all need help in how to handle it.

FACE-TO-FACE

You can end up spending so much time on your favourite sites that you may forget to actually meet people face-to-face! Once you start spending time with your friends, you'll soon realise how much more enjoyable it is to talk and properly experience being together, instead of everyone being glued to their phones all the time.

TRY THIS!

Set yourself a tech break challenge. Try and stick to only an hour a day on social media. Or switch it off completely for a whole weekend or a week. It might seem a bit strange at first, but think about all the other things you can do instead!

THE LAST WORD – SELFIES!

We all do it – with our best friends, family and pets. Selfies can be great, but you need to be careful about which people you share them with.

SPECIAL MOMENTS

Posting pictures of yourself online to share special moments with your friends and family is a great way to keep in touch and create memories for years to come. However be careful when you post selfies.

Showing your best friend or granny your latest holiday photos of you on the beach in your swimming gear or wearing your favourite pyjamas is fine, but make sure you don't send personal photos to everyone you're linked to online. Be aware that people you don't know that well may make comments that could make you feel bad – and no one needs that!

SHARE WITH CARE

When you post pictures of yourself online you have no control of where they end up or who can get hold of them. What seems funny and cute to share with your friends now might be embarrassing when you're older. Think about what you're posting online ... if you wouldn't want your parents, teachers, carers or the whole school to see it, don't post it! When you do share selfies, make sure it's just with your close friends and family, not with people you don't know that well.

GLOSSARY

ADDICTIVE
describes something that becomes a habit that someone feels they can't live without

ANOREXIA
an emotional illness where someone stops eating because they believe they are overweight

ANXIOUS
describes the feeling of being worried, nervous or uneasy

BINGE EATING
an emotional illness where someone eats huge amounts of food in a short period of time

BODY IMAGE
how someone sees their body and how they think it should look

BULIMIA
an emotional illness where someone eats too much and then makes themselves sick or stops eating

CELLS
tiny organisms that make up a living body

CONFIDENCE
belief in yourself and your ability to do things

CONFUSED
not thinking clearly

CYBERBULLYING
being called names or threatened online or being deliberately excluded from online activities

ENVIOUS
describes the feeling of wanting what someone else has got

EXCLUDED
left out, not included

GROWTH HORMONES
substances released into the body that help it to grow and develop

HUMILIATE
make a person feel stupid and embarrassed in front of other people

IMMUNE SYSTEME
the part of the body that protects us from diseases

MENTAL HEALTH
how someone thinks about their life, their emotions and how they feel about themselves

NEGATIVE FEELINGS
feelings that are bad, such as not liking the way you look and thinking you are stupid

NERVOUS SYSTEM
the part of the body made up of the brain and spinal cord that uses signals to help us to move, communicate, receive information and make sense of the world around us

OBSESS
think about something non-stop

OVERWHELMING
describes the experience that a situation or feeling is too big or too difficult to handle

POSITIVE
describes feeling good, confident and able to cope

PRAISE
tell someone they've done something well

PSYCHOLOGISTS
experts that study and understand why people think and behave in a certain way

PUBERTY
the time when the body starts to develop to become an adult

SELF-ESTEEM
the way you feel about yourself and your belief in what you can achieve

SELF-WORTH
the sense of how you value and respect yourself

STRESS
the emotional and mental strain when it feels as if everything is getting too much

WORTHLESS
describes something of no value

43

NOTES FOR TEACHERS, PARENTS AND CARERS

It is important to recognise early on the signs of young people who may be suffering from obsessive use of social media or cyberbullying. The online survey 'Digital Friendships – the role of technology in young people's relationships', found that around a quarter to over half of the 2,000 children surveyed said that adults didn't understand their online lives.

TEACHERS, LOOK OUT FOR:

* usually outgoing, bright students being sleepy all the time, losing concentration in class, getting bad results or not doing their homework properly or at all
* students with a good attendance record not turning up for school
* students becoming withdrawn and anxious.

WHAT TO DO:

* Does the school have a 'no personal devices on the premises' policy? If not, consider implementing one. Students can hand in their devices at the office and collect them at the end of the day.
* Talk to the class as a whole about social media safely and discuss privacy settings. Be positive about social media, but explain that interacting with each other face-to-face is just as important as online communication.
* Talk to students about why social media is important to them and how they use it.
* Discuss cyberbullying, what it is and how it affects people. Does the school have an anti-bullying policy? If it does, discuss this at assembly. If it doesn't, talk to your colleagues about putting one together. At assembly, ask the students for ideas.
* Discuss the positives and negatives of online relationships and how these can be managed.

* Suggest various scenarios and ask the students to discuss them. For example, is it possible to become obsessed with instant messaging, does it matter who sees your online photos? Have a debate with a 'for' and 'against' team.
It is important for students to think through for themselves the problems that can arise; that way they will be better equipped to deal with them.
* Have a noticeboard where helplines and support groups can be displayed.
* Have a safe space where students can talk to a teacher about any issues they are having.
* Make sure students know that teachers are not going to be angry or judgmental that they are using social media while under age.
* Get creative. Write and perform a play as a class about someone becoming obsessed with social media. Perhaps the play could include a scene with one of the students acting as a counsellor.

FOR PARENTS AND CARERS

If you are worried that your child is spending too much time on social media talk to them about your concerns, and ask whether they feel the same. You may find they agree with you, but are finding it difficult to manage their time online. Go through this book with your child and discuss the issues raised. Ask questions gently to encourage your child to open up and let them take the lead in the conversation. If you feel your child is developing a dependence on social media, mental health issues or being cyberbullied, speak to their school, your doctor or contact a helpline (see pages 46-47).

FURTHER INFORMATION

WEBSITES AND HELPLINES

If you feel overwhelmed by any of the issues you've read about in this book, or need advice, check out a website or call a helpline and talk to someone who will understand.

www.childline.org.uk/info-advice/your-feelings/mental-health
Find out about mental health issues, meet others, message or call the 24-hour helpline for advice or someone who'll just listen.
Telephone: 0800 1111

www.samaritans.org
A place where anyone can go for advice and comfort. The helpline number is 116 123.

www.sane.org/get-help
Help and support for anyone affected by mental and emotional issues.
The helpline number is 0300 304 7000.

www.supportline.org.uk
A charity giving emotional support to children and young people.
The helpline number is 01708 765200.

www.childnet.com
This organisation helps children and young people to stay safe online and shares advice with teachers, parents and carers, too.

www.youngminds.org.uk
Information and advice for children and young people experiencing bullying, stress and mental or emotional anxieties.

https://www.brainline.org/article/who-me-self-esteem-people-disabilities
How to boost self-esteem regardless of disabilities.

AUSTRALIA AND NEW ZEALAND

www.healthdirect.gov.au/partners/kids-helpline
A helpline for young people giving advice,
counselling and support.
The number is 1800 55 1800.

www.kidsline.org.nz
Helpline run by specially trained young volunteers
to help kids and teens deal with troubling issues
and problems. The number is 0800 54 37 54.

Note to parents and teachers: every effort has been made
by the Publishers to ensure that these websites are suitable
for children, that they are of the highest educational value,
and that they contain no inappropriate or offensive material.
However, because of the nature of the Internet, it is impossible
to guarantee that the contents of these sites will not be altered.
We strongly advise that Internet access is supervised by a
responsible adult.

BOOKS

Positively Teenage
Nicola Morgan, Franklin Watts, 2018

Dr Christian's Guide to Growing Up Online
Dr Christian Jessen, Scholastic, 2018

Texts, Tweets, Trolls and Teens
Anita Naik, Wayland, 2014

INDEX

abuse 29
alone 14, 20, 34
anxious 5, 8, 9, 14, 29, 31, 37, 38
ashamed 35

bad 14, 36
body image 22, 23, 26
bullied 5, 14, 28, 29, 30

confused 14
cross 37

depressed 8, 9, 29, 31
dissatisfied 19
dreams 32

eating disorders 22
embarrassed 35
envious 19
excited 8
excluded 8, 13, 14, 15

fear of missing out (FOMO) 5,
   10, 12

good 8, 25, 26
groggy 32, 33
grumpy 31
guilty 35

happy 8, 11, 16, 30
hopeless 9
hurt 5

in control 6
inspired 8, 27
isolated 9, 20

jealous 5, 15
joy 16

left out 13
lonely 9, 20
low self-esteem 12

miserable 26

not good enough 5, 17

out of control 12

panicky 38
positive 15, 17, 18, 26, 27
puberty 22

sad 8, 9, 14, 34
scared 5, 34
self-esteem 17, 22
self-harming 29
selfies 40, 41
self-worth 25, 26
shocked 13, 25
sleep 31, 32, 33
stressed 12, 19, 37
stupid 17
supported 8

tech break challenge 37, 39
tired 11

ugly 17
unable to concentrate 31
unhappy 5, 19, 23
upset 5, 14

withdrawn 29
worried 8, 35, 38
worthless 17

ISBN 978 1 4451 6451 9 (HB); 978 1 4451 6452 6 (PB)

* What is stress?
* Stress test
* Coping with stress
* What is anxiety?
* What if ...?
* Good thinking!
* Stress at home
* Making friends
* Panic attacks
* Routines and rituals
* Help at home
* Enjoy life
* The last word – positivity

ISBN 978 1 4451 6473 1 (HB); 978 1 4451 6474 8 (PB)

* Social media, it's great, right?
* Social media and your brain
* Oh, no! FOMO!
* Exclusion zone
* Please like me!
* Not real life
* Body image
* Developing self-worth
* Cyberbullying
* Sleep well
* Online help
* Take a tech break
* The last word – selfies!

ISBN 978 1 4451 6471 7 (HB); 978 1 4451 6472 4 (PB)

* Dream team!
* Hello, brain!
* Hormone havoc!
* Eat well
* Issues with eating
* Self-esteem
* Body image
* Sweet dreams!
* Always tired
* What's so good about exercise?
* Be positive!
* A healthy future
* The last word – mindfulness

ISBN 978 1 4451 6469 4 (HB); 978 1 4451 6470 0 (PB)

* What are emotions?
* Emotional chaos
* What else affects moods?
* Emotions and thoughts
* Emotions and behaviour
* Sweaty palms and a red face!
* Feeling sad
* Feeling happy
* Feeling angry
* Feeling scared
* Relationships
* Friends for life
* The last word – me!